A Concise History of Human Migration

Barry Richardson

Published by Barry Richardson, 2026.

A CONCISE HISTORY OF HUMAN MIGRATION

First edition. January 28, 2026.

ISBN: 979-8232329396

Written by Barry Richardson.

Table of Contents

Introduction: Why Humans Move

Imagine a small band of people standing at the edge of a savannah, tens of thousands of years ago. The rains have failed, the herds have wandered elsewhere and the horizon promises both uncertainty and possibility. They gather what they can carry - tools, fire, memory - and step forward. That moment, repeated countless times across millennia, is the essence of human migration: the decision to move, to seek, to hope – to survive.

Migration is not an exception in human history; it is the rule. From the first footsteps out of Africa to the crowded airports of today, people have been on the move. Sometimes the reasons are stark - famine, war or persecution. Sometimes they are aspirational - trade, adventure, love or the dream of a better life. At other times, movement is simply woven into the rhythms of existence: nomads following the seasons, pilgrims tracing sacred paths or families drifting toward opportunity.

The forces that drive migration are sometimes described as "push" and "pull". Push factors are the pressures that compel departure, such as hunger, conflict or environmental change. Pull factors are the attractions that beckon: fertile land, bustling cities, safety, prosperity. Yet behind these terms lies something more profound - the human capacity to imagine life elsewhere and the courage to pursue it.

Migration is also a story of encounter. Every movement brings people into contact with new landscapes, new cultures and new ideas. Sometimes these encounters spark flourishing exchange; sometimes they ignite conflict. But always, they reshape identities, languages and traditions. The foods we eat, the words we speak, the beliefs we hold - all bear the imprint of journeys taken long before us.

This book tells the story of those journeys. It begins with the earliest dispersals of our species and follows the great arcs of movement across continents and centuries. It traces the migrations that built civilisations, spread religions, fuelled empires and transformed economies.

It explores the forced migrations of slavery and exile, the hopeful migrations of labour and settlement and the urgent migrations of refugees fleeing danger. It also looks ahead to the migrations of tomorrow, driven by climate change, technology and global interconnection.

To understand human migration is to understand ourselves. We are, at heart, a migratory species - restless, resilient and imaginative. Our history is written in footprints across deserts, in ships crossing oceans, in caravans along trade routes and in planes soaring above continents. This is the human journey: a story of movement, of survival and of belonging.

Chapter 1: Out of Africa

Long before cities, kingdoms or written words existed, humanity's greatest journey began with a single step out of Africa. For hundreds of thousands of years our ancestors lived exclusively on that vast continent, adapting to its savannah, forests and deserts. Africa was not just the *birthplace* of Homo sapiens - it was the crucible in which our species learned to survive, innovate and imagine. Yet around 60,000-70,000 years ago, a small group of humans decided to leave, setting in motion the migrations that would eventually populate the entire globe.

The African Homeland

The story begins deep in prehistory. Fossil evidence shows that early hominins - our evolutionary cousins - thrived in Africa for millions of years. Homo erectus, Homo habilis and other species walked the same landscapes long before Homo sapiens appeared.

By about 200,000 years ago, anatomically modern humans had emerged in East Africa. They were hunter-gatherers, living in small bands, using stone tools, fire and language to coordinate survival. Africa's diversity of environments - from the Rift Valley to the Sahara - shaped their resilience and adaptability.

The First Steps Beyond

The earliest migrations out of Africa may have occurred in waves. Some groups ventured into the Middle East as early as 120,000 years ago, following favourable climates and abundant game. Archaeological sites in Israel, such as Skhul and Qafzeh caves, preserve remains of these pioneers. Yet these early excursions were not permanent. Climate shifts and competition may have forced them back, leaving Africa as the enduring centre of human life.

The decisive migration came later, around 60,000–70,000 years ago. Genetic studies trace the ancestry of all non-African populations to a relatively small group that crossed out of Africa during this period. They likely travelled along the Red Sea coast, crossing into the Arabian Peninsula. From there, they spread eastward and northward, hugging coastlines and river valleys that offered food and shelter.

Encounters with Other Hominins

As humans moved into new lands, they were not alone. Neanderthals lived across Europe and western Asia, while Denisovans occupied parts of Asia. These encounters were not merely confrontations - they were moments of contact, exchange and even interbreeding.

Genetic evidence reveals that modern humans carry traces of Neanderthal and Denisovan DNA, a reminder that migration was not only about dispersal but also about blending. These encounters enriched the genetic diversity of our species and may have conferred advantages in immunity and adaptation.

Following the Coasts

One of the great mysteries of early migration is how quickly humans spread. Evidence suggests that coastal routes played a crucial role. By following shorelines, humans could rely on fishing, shellfish gathering and predictable resources. This "beachcomber strategy" may explain how humans reached South Asia and Southeast Asia within a few thousand years of leaving Africa. Archaeological finds in caves along the Indian Ocean rim show early settlements, tools and art that testify to this rapid expansion.

Perhaps the most astonishing achievement of early migration was the settlement of Australia. By 50,000 years ago, humans had crossed through Southeast Asia and reached the continent, despite the need to navigate open water. This required not only physical endurance but also technological ingenuity - rafts or boats capable of carrying families across treacherous seas. Once in Australia, humans adapted to deserts, forests and coasts, leaving behind rock art and cultural traditions that endure to this day.

The peopling of the Americas came much later but its roots lie in the same Out of Africa dispersal. Around 15,000–20,000 years ago, humans crossed into the Americas via this land bridge, beginning another chapter of migration that would shape entire continents. But the foundation of this journey was laid in Africa, when those first bands of humans stepped beyond familiar horizons.

The Legacy of Departure

The Out of Africa migration was more than a physical movement - it was a turning point in human history. It demonstrated our species' capacity for exploration, adaptation and imagination. Each step carried not only bodies but also stories, languages and traditions. The echoes of that migration live on in our DNA, in the diversity of cultures across the world and in the shared truth that all humans, no matter where they live today, can trace their origins back to Africa.

Chapter 2: Settling the Continents

When small bands of humans first stepped beyond Africa, they carried with them not only tools and fire but also the seeds of global history. Over tens of thousands of years, these groups fanned out across the continents, adapting to new climates, inventing new ways of life and leaving traces of their journeys in bones, artefacts and stories. The settling of the continents was not a single event but a series of overlapping migrations, each shaped by geography, climate and human ingenuity.

Asia: The First Great Expansion

Asia was humanity's first great frontier beyond Africa. By 60,000 years ago, humans had reached the Arabian Peninsula and spread eastward into South Asia. Archaeological sites in India reveal stone tools and hearths that mark their presence. Genetic studies suggest that South Asia became a major crossroads, where populations mixed and diversified.

From there, humans moved into Southeast Asia, following rivers and coastlines. The tropical forests posed new challenges - dense vegetation, unfamiliar diseases and dangerous predators - but humans adapted, developing new hunting strategies and exploiting rich coastal resources. By 50,000 years ago, they had reached the islands of Indonesia and the Philippines, evidence of early seafaring skills.

Australia: Crossing the Seas

One of the most remarkable achievements of early migration was the settlement of Australia. To reach it, humans had to cross stretches of open water, even during Ice Age periods when sea levels were lower. This required boats or rafts, as well as the ability to navigate by stars, currents

and memory. By 50,000 years ago, humans were living in Australia, leaving behind rock art that still speaks across millennia.

Australia's landscapes demanded extraordinary adaptability. In the arid interior, survival meant mastering water sources and seasonal cycles. Along the coasts, fishing and shellfish gathering sustained communities. Aboriginal traditions, passed down orally for tens of thousands of years, preserve memories of these early migrations and of landscapes that have since vanished beneath rising seas.

Europe: Meeting the Neanderthals

While humans were settling Asia and Australia, other groups moved north into Europe. By 45,000 years ago, they had reached the continent, entering lands already occupied by Neanderthals. The meeting of these two species was complex - sometimes competitive, sometimes cooperative and occasionally intimate. Genetic evidence shows that interbreeding occurred, leaving Neanderthal DNA in modern populations.

Europe's Ice Age climate posed immense challenges. Vast glaciers covered much of the land, and survival required clothing, shelter and fire. Humans developed tailored clothing from animal hides, built sturdy shelters and created art that reflected both survival and imagination. The cave paintings of Lascaux and Chauvet, dating back more than 30,000 years, testify to a flourishing of symbolic thought during this period.

The Americas: Crossing Beringia

The last great frontier was the Americas. During the Ice Age, a land bridge known as Beringia connected Siberia to Alaska. Around 15,000–20,000 years ago, humans crossed this bridge, following herds of mammoth and bison. Some scholars argue for earlier arrivals, perhaps by coastal routes but the evidence remains debated.

Once in the Americas, humans spread rapidly. Within a few thousand years, they had reached South America, adapting to deserts, mountains and rainforests. Archaeological sites such as Monte Verde in Chile show human presence as early as 14,500 years ago. These migrations laid the foundation for the great civilisations of the Americas - Maya, Aztec and Inca - centuries later.

The Pacific Islands: Voyages of Discovery

The settlement of the Pacific Islands represents another extraordinary chapter. Beginning around 3,000 years ago, Austronesian peoples developed advanced seafaring technologies - outrigger canoes, navigation by stars and currents - that allowed them to cross vast stretches of ocean. They settled islands from Polynesia to Micronesia, creating cultures that thrived in isolation yet remained connected by shared traditions of voyaging.

These migrations were not random wanderings but deliberate acts of exploration. Oral traditions describe navigators who memorised the patterns of waves, winds and birds to find distant islands. The settlement of places like Hawaii, New Zealand and Easter Island stands as a testament to human daring and ingenuity.

The Human Web

By the end of these migrations, humanity had settled every habitable continent. Each journey left its mark: genetic diversity, cultural traditions and technological innovations. The settling of the continents was not merely about survival - it was about creating new worlds. From the tundras of Siberia to the deserts of Australia, humans transformed landscapes and were transformed by them.

This chapter of migration reminds us that humanity's story is one of movement and adaptation. The continents we inhabit today were claimed through courage, resilience and imagination. In every corner of the globe, echoes of those journeys remain - in languages, myths and the very DNA of our bodies.

Chapter 3: Ancient Civilisations and Trade Routes

As humans settled the continents, they began to cluster in fertile valleys, along rivers and near coasts where agriculture could flourish. These settlements grew into villages, then cities and eventually civilisations. With civilisation came new forms of migration - not just survival-driven dispersals but purposeful movements shaped by trade, conquest and cultural exchange. The ancient world was a web of journeys, connecting distant peoples through roads, rivers and seas.

The Nile and the Birth of Egypt

The Nile River was more than a waterway; it was a lifeline. Each year, its floods deposited rich silt that sustained agriculture. Communities migrated along its banks, drawn by fertile land and reliable harvests. Over time, these settlements coalesced into one of the world's first great civilisations: Egypt.

Migration here was not only internal. The Nile connected Egypt to Nubia in the south and the Mediterranean in the north. Traders, soldiers and artisans moved along its length, carrying gold, ivory and ideas. Egypt's pyramids and temples were built not just by locals but by workers drawn from across its empire, a testament to how migration fuelled monumental achievement.

Mesopotamia: The Crossroads of Peoples

Between the Tigris and Euphrates rivers lay Mesopotamia, often called the "cradle of civilisation" Here, Sumerians, Akkadians, Babylonians and Assyrians rose and fell, each leaving its mark. Migration was constant

- farmers moving to fertile plains, merchants travelling between cities, conquerors expanding empires.

Mesopotamia's position made it a crossroads. Caravans brought goods from India, Anatolia and the Levant. Ideas flowed with them in the forms of writing, mathematics and astronomy. The famous Code of Hammurabi, one of the earliest legal systems, reflects a society shaped by diverse peoples living side by side.

The Indus Valley: A Forgotten Network

Farther east, the Indus Valley civilisation thrived around 2500 BC. Cities such as Mohenjo-Daro and Harappa were marvels of urban planning, with grid streets and advanced drainage systems. Migration here was tied to trade: beads, cotton and pottery moved across regions, linking the Indus to Mesopotamia and beyond.

Although the civilisation eventually declined, perhaps due to climate shifts or river changes, its legacy reminds us that migration is not only about expansion but also about resilience and adaptation. When rivers dried or floods failed, people moved, seeking new lands to sustain their lives.

The Silk Road: Threads Across Continents

Perhaps the most famous ancient trade route was the Silk Road, stretching thousands of miles from China to the Mediterranean. It was not a single road but a network of paths, caravan trails and sea routes. Along it travelled silk, spices, precious metals and glass - but also religions, technologies and diseases.

Merchants, pilgrims and envoys migrated along these routes, creating cosmopolitan cities such as Samarkand and Kashgar. Buddhism spread from India into China; Christianity and Islam later travelled eastward.

The Silk Road was a living artery of migration, binding distant civilisations into a shared story.

Migration Through Conquest

Not all ancient migrations were peaceful. Empires expanded through conquest, moving armies and populations across vast territories. Alexander the Great's campaigns carried Greek culture into Egypt, Persia and India. The Roman Empire drew peoples from Britain to Syria into its orbit, relocating soldiers, slaves and settlers.

These migrations reshaped identities. Roman roads and aqueducts connected distant provinces, while Latin and Greek became *lingua francas*. Conquered peoples often blended their traditions with those of their rulers, creating hybrid cultures that endured long after empires fell.

Maritime Migrations

The seas were highways of migration. Phoenician sailors ventured across the Mediterranean, founding colonies and spreading their alphabet. Greek city-states sent settlers to Italy, Turkey and North Africa. Later, Arab traders crossed the Indian Ocean, linking East Africa with India and Southeast Asia.

These maritime migrations were driven by trade but also by curiosity and necessity. Ships carried not only goods but also families, languages and gods. Ports became melting pots where cultures mingled and migration by sea became a defining feature of the ancient world.

The Human Web of Antiquity

By the end of antiquity, humanity had woven a dense web of connections. Migration was no longer just about survival - it was about building civilisations, exchanging knowledge and shaping identities.

Ancient trade routes carried more than commodities; they carried the essence of human culture.

The story of ancient migration is the story of how isolated communities became interconnected worlds. It is the story of how roads, rivers and seas turned human movement into civilisation itself.

Chapter 4: Faith, Pilgrimage and Diaspora

Migration is not only about survival or trade - it is also about belief. Across centuries, faith has inspired people to move: to seek sacred places, to escape persecution, to spread teachings or to preserve identity in exile. Pilgrimage and diaspora are two of the most powerful forms of migration, shaping cultures and communities across the world.

Pilgrimage: Journeys of the Spirit

Pilgrimage is one of humanity's oldest forms of migration. It is a journey not for conquest or commerce but for devotion. Pilgrims walk, ride or sail toward places believed to hold divine presence, carrying with them prayers, hopes and sacrifices.

➢ **Christian Pilgrimages**: From the early centuries, Christians travelled to Jerusalem, Bethlehem and Rome. The medieval pilgrimage to Santiago de Compostela in Spain drew thousands across Europe, creating networks of inns, chapels and roads. Pilgrimage was both a spiritual act and a social phenomenon, binding communities together.

➢ **Islamic Pilgrimage**: The Hajj to Mecca is one of the Five Pillars of Islam, a sacred duty for Muslims who are able to undertake it. For centuries, caravans crossed deserts and seas to reach the Kaaba, transforming Mecca into a global meeting point of cultures. Even today, millions gather annually, making the Hajj one of the largest migrations on earth.

- ➢ **Buddhist Pilgrimages**: Followers of the Buddha journeyed to sites associated with his life - Lumbini, Bodh Gaya, Sarnath and Kushinagar. These pilgrimages spread Buddhism across Asia, linking distant communities through shared devotion.

- ➢ **Hindu Pilgrimages**: In India, rivers, temples and mountains became sacred destinations. The Kumbh Mela, held at the confluence of holy rivers, remains one of the largest gatherings of humans in history, a testament to the enduring power of pilgrimage.

Pilgrimage routes became arteries of culture. Along them flowed not only faith but also art, music and commerce. Pilgrims carried stories home, enriching their communities with new traditions and perspectives.

Diaspora: Scattering and Survival

If pilgrimage is voluntary, diaspora is often forced. Diaspora refers to communities scattered from their homelands, often through persecution, conquest or economic necessity. Yet diasporas are not only stories of loss - they are also stories of resilience.

- ➢ **The Jewish Diaspora**: One of the most enduring examples, the Jewish people were exiled from their homeland multiple times - by Babylonian conquest, Roman destruction and medieval expulsions. Yet wherever they settled, they preserved identity through language, ritual and memory. Synagogues became centres of community and the dream of return remained alive across centuries.

- ➢ **Christian Migrations**: Early Christians often fled persecution in the Roman Empire, spreading their faith as they moved. Later, sects such as the Puritans migrated to the Americas, seeking freedom to practise their beliefs. Their journeys shaped new societies built on religious ideals.

➢ **Muslim Diasporas**: The spread of Islam was both voluntary and forced. Traders carried Islam across Africa and Asia, while persecution sometimes displaced communities. In Spain, after the Reconquista, Muslims were expelled or forced to convert, creating diasporas that carried their traditions elsewhere.

➢ **Other Diasporas**: Armenians, Zoroastrians, Sikhs and countless others experienced displacement. Each diaspora carried with it a unique blend of memory and adaptation, preserving identity while reshaping it in new lands.

Diasporas often became bridges between cultures. Jewish merchants linked Europe and the Middle East; Armenian traders connected Asia and the Mediterranean. Diaspora communities preserved traditions while also absorbing influences from their host societies, creating hybrid cultures that enriched the world.

Faith as a Force of Migration

Faith-driven migration is not only about leaving - it is about belonging. Pilgrims return home transformed, carrying new perspectives. Diaspora communities build new homes while keeping alive the memory of old ones. In both cases, migration becomes a way of sustaining identity across distance and time.

Faith also reshaped geography. Pilgrimage routes carved paths across continents; diasporas created networks of communities that spanned oceans. Shrines, temples, mosques and churches became magnets of movement, drawing people across borders and generations.

The Human Dimension

Behind every pilgrimage and diaspora are human stories: a mother carrying her child to a sacred river, a family fleeing persecution with only their faith to sustain them, a community rebuilding identity in exile. These stories remind us that migration is not only about bodies moving across space - it is about hearts and minds seeking meaning, safety and belonging.

Faith, pilgrimage and diaspora reveal migration as more than a physical act. They show it as a spiritual journey, a quest for identity and a testament to resilience. In the next chapter, we turn to **Medieval Migrations**, where exploration, conquest and commerce reshaped the world in ways that would set the stage for the modern age.

Chapter 5: Medieval Migrations

The medieval era was a time of movement as dynamic as any age before it. Although often imagined as static centuries of castles and feudal villages, the Middle Ages were alive with journeys. Explorers crossed seas, nomads swept across steppes, merchants threaded through markets and scholars travelled between centres of learning. Migration in this period had the added dimensions of expansion, curiosity and the weaving together of worlds.

Viking Voyages: Raiders and Settlers

From the fjords of Scandinavia, the Vikings set out in sleek longships that could navigate both open seas and shallow rivers. Beginning in the 8th century, they raided monasteries and towns across Europe, striking terror into coastal communities. Yet their migrations were not only violent incursions - they were also acts of settlement and trade.

- **Settlements**: Vikings established colonies in Iceland, Greenland and even reached North America around the year 1000, landing at L'Anse aux Meadows in Newfoundland. These journeys represent some of the earliest European crossings of the Atlantic.

- **Integration**: In England, France and Ireland, Viking settlers blended with local populations, leaving behind language, law and cultural traditions. The city of Dublin, for example, began as a Viking trading post.

- ➢ **Commerce**: Viking merchants carried furs, amber and slaves across Europe, linking northern lands to the Mediterranean and beyond.

The Viking migrations remind us that movement can be both destructive and creative, reshaping societies through encounter and exchange.

The Mongol Expansions: A World Connected

In the 13th century, the Mongols under Genghis Khan unleashed one of the most dramatic migrations in history. Nomadic horsemen from the steppes of Central Asia swept across Eurasia, conquering vast territories from China to Eastern Europe.

- ➢ **Military Migration**: Mongol armies moved with astonishing speed, carrying entire communities across continents. Their campaigns displaced populations but also created new networks of movement.

- ➢ **Cultural Exchange**: The Mongol Empire became a conduit for trade and ideas. The Pax Mongolica - "Mongol Peace" - allowed merchants, missionaries and travellers to move safely across Eurasia. Marco Polo's journey to China was made possible by these conditions.

- ➢ **Diversity**: The empire absorbed Persians, Chinese, Russians and countless others, creating a mosaic of cultures under Mongol rule.

Although often remembered for conquest, the Mongol migrations also knit together distant worlds, laying foundations for global connections that would endure.

Merchants and Markets: The Rise of Medieval Trade

Medieval Europe saw the growth of towns and markets, fuelled by merchant migrations. Traders moved along rivers and roads, carrying wool, wine, salt and spices. The Hanseatic League, a network of trading cities around the Baltic and North Seas, exemplified how migration of merchants could create powerful economic alliances.

➢ **Fairs and Exchanges**: Annual fairs in places like Champagne drew merchants from across Europe, creating temporary hubs of migration where cultures mingled.

➢ **Long-Distance Trade**: Italian merchants from Venice and Genoa sailed to the Levant, linking Europe to the Middle East. Their journeys brought silk, spices and knowledge back to Europe, sparking cultural transformation.

These migrations of merchants were not only economic - they were cultural, introducing new foods, fashions and ideas into medieval life.

Scholars and Pilgrims: Journeys of the Mind and Spirit

Medieval migrations were also intellectual and spiritual. Scholars travelled to centres of learning such as Baghdad, Cordoba and Paris seeking knowledge in philosophy, medicine and theology. Their journeys spread ideas across continents, preserving ancient wisdom and sparking new discoveries.

Pilgrimage continued to thrive. Christians walked to Santiago de Compostela, Canterbury and Rome. Muslims journeyed to Mecca for the Hajj. These pilgrimages created networks of roads, inns and shrines, sustaining communities and economies along the way.

The Crusades: Faith and Conflict

Beginning in the late 11th century, the Crusades mobilised vast migrations of knights, peasants and pilgrims from Europe to the Holy

Land. These journeys were driven by faith, ambition and the promise of salvation. While the Crusades brought violence and upheaval, they also opened channels of exchange between Europe and the Middle East.

Crusaders returned with new foods, technologies and ideas - spices, sugar, algebra and medical knowledge. Migration through conflict reshaped Europe's horizons, expanding its awareness of distant lands and cultures.

The Medieval Mosaic

By the end of the Middle Ages, migration had transformed the world. Vikings had crossed oceans, Mongols had united continents, merchants had built networks of trade and pilgrims had walked paths of devotion. The medieval era was not static - it was a mosaic of movement, encounters and exchanges.

Migration in this period reminds us that even in times of castles and kingdoms, humanity was restless, curious and interconnected. The journeys of the medieval world set the stage for the next great age of migration: the Age of Exploration, when ships would cross oceans and empires would span the globe.

Chapter 6: The Age of Exploration

By the fifteenth century, humanity stood on the brink of a new era. The medieval world had already been knit together by trade routes, pilgrimages and conquests but now ships would carry people farther than ever before. The Age of Exploration expanded migrations on a global scale.

Europeans crossed oceans, Indigenous peoples were displaced, Africans were enslaved and transported and new societies emerged from the mingling and clashing of cultures. Migration in this age was both voluntary and forced, hopeful and tragic, transformative and devastating.

European Voyages: Expanding Horizons

The Age of Exploration began with curiosity and ambition. Portuguese sailors, guided by Prince Henry the Navigator, ventured down the coast of Africa, seeking gold, spices and a route to India. In 1492, Christopher Columbus sailed westward, reaching the Caribbean and opening the Americas to European expansion. Soon, explorers such as Vasco da Gama, Ferdinand Magellan and Hernán Cortés carried European flags across oceans and continents.

These voyages were migrations in themselves. Crews of sailors, soldiers and settlers left their homelands for distant shores. Colonies sprang up in the Americas, Africa and Asia, populated by Europeans seeking land, wealth or religious freedom. Migration became a tool of empire, reshaping the demographics of entire continents.

The Transatlantic Slave Trade: Forced Migration

No migration of this era was more tragic than the transatlantic slave trade. Beginning in the 16th century, millions of Africans were captured, sold and transported across the Atlantic to work on plantations in the Americas. This forced migration tore families apart, devastated communities and reshaped Africa's demographic landscape.

The Middle Passage - the journey across the Atlantic - was a nightmare of overcrowding, disease and death. Yet even in the face of unimaginable suffering, enslaved Africans carried with them languages, traditions and spiritual practices that would endure and transform cultures in the Americas. The African diaspora became one of the most significant migrations in human history, its legacy still felt today.

Indigenous Displacement: The Other Side of Exploration

For Indigenous peoples of the Americas, the arrival of Europeans brought upheaval. Migration here was not voluntary but imposed. Communities were displaced from ancestral lands, forced into missions or decimated by disease. Entire populations migrated under duress, seeking refuge from conquest and colonisation.

Yet Indigenous resilience persisted. Some groups adapted by moving into new territories, others resisted through warfare and many preserved traditions in spite of displacement. Migration in this context was survival against overwhelming odds.

Cultural Transformation: Mixing Worlds

The Age of Exploration created new societies through migration and encounter. Europeans, Africans and Indigenous peoples mingled, sometimes violently, sometimes creatively. Languages blended, cuisines fused and religions adapted. In Latin America, Mestizo populations emerged from the mixing of European and Indigenous ancestry. In the Caribbean, African traditions shaped music, dance and spirituality.

Migration also carried crops and animals across continents. Potatoes and maize travelled from the Americas to Europe; horses and cattle crossed from Europe to the New World. This "Columbian Exchange" transformed diets, economies and environments worldwide, a migration of species alongside people.

Global Networks

By the end of the Age of Exploration, the world was connected as never before. Migration had created colonies, diasporas and hybrid cultures. Oceans were no longer barriers but highways of movement. The migrations of this era were often brutal but they also laid the foundations for the modern global system.

The Human Cost and Legacy

The Age of Exploration reminds us that migration is not always a story of freedom. It can be a story of coercion, exploitation and loss. Yet it also shows humanity's capacity to adapt, to create new identities and to forge connections across vast distances. The migrations of this era reshaped continents, economies and cultures, leaving a legacy that continues to define our world.

Chapter 7: Industrial Revolutions and Urban Migration

The Industrial Revolution was not only a technological upheaval - it was a migration revolution. Steam engines, factories and mechanised agriculture transformed the rhythms of life, pulling millions from rural villages into booming cities and pushing millions more across oceans in search of opportunity. Migration in this era was both voluntary and compelled, driven by the promise of work, the pressures of poverty and the lure of new worlds.

From Fields to Factories

For centuries, most people lived in rural communities, tied to the land through farming. The Industrial Revolution shattered this pattern. In Britain, mechanised looms and steam-powered mills created demand for labour in cities such as Manchester, Birmingham and London. Families left ancestral villages, carrying little more than hope, to crowd into smoky urban neighbourhoods.

This rural-to-urban migration was not unique to Britain. Across Europe, peasants abandoned fields for factories, reshaping demographics. Cities swelled as their populations doubled or tripled within decades. Migration created new urban cultures - working-class neighbourhoods, bustling markets and social movements that demanded rights and reforms.

Across the Atlantic: Mass Migration to the Americas

Industrialisation also fuelled transatlantic migration. Between the mid-19th and early 20th centuries, tens of millions of Europeans crossed the ocean to the Americas. Irish families fled famine, Italians sought work, Germans pursued land and Eastern Europeans escaped persecution. Ellis Island in New York became a symbol of this migration, processing millions of arrivals who would build new lives in the United States.

South America, too, became a destination. Argentina, Brazil and Chile welcomed immigrants to work in agriculture, railroads and industry. Migration reshaped these societies, blending European traditions with local cultures and Indigenous heritage.

Labour Migrations: Building New Worlds

Industrial economies demanded labour and migration supplied it. In the United States, Chinese workers built railroads across the West, while African Americans migrated north during the Great Migration, seeking factory jobs and escaping racial violence in the South. In Europe, rural migrants filled factories, while colonial subjects were recruited to work in imperial centres.

These migrations were often fraught with hardship. Immigrants faced discrimination, poor housing and dangerous working conditions. Yet they also built communities such as Chinatowns, Little Italys and Jewish quarters - that preserved their identities while adapting to new realities. Migration created the mosaic of modern cities, where cultures coexisted, clashed and blended.

Urban Transformation

The influx of migrants transformed cities. Streets filled with languages from across the world; markets offered foods from distant homelands. Churches, synagogues, mosques and temples rose to serve diverse communities. Migration made cities cosmopolitan, hubs of innovation and creativity.

But urban migration also brought challenges. Overcrowding, pollution and poverty plagued industrial cities. Reformers and governments struggled to provide housing, sanitation and education. Migration forced societies to confront the realities of modernisation, shaping policies and institutions that endure today.

The Human Story

Behind the statistics are human stories: a farmer's daughter leaving her village for a textile mill, a family boarding a ship to America with dreams of land, a labourer crossing borders to build railroads. Migration in the industrial age was about survival and opportunity but also about identity - how people carried traditions into new worlds and forged new communities in the heart of cities.

The Legacy

By the end of the industrial era, migration had reshaped the global map. Cities became magnets of humanity, drawing millions into their orbit. Nations were transformed by immigrant populations, their cultures enriched and challenged by diversity. Migration in this age was as much about the creation of modern society as it was about movement.

Chapter 8: War, Refugees and Resettlement

If the Industrial Revolution drew millions into cities and across oceans, the wars of the 20th century scattered them again. Conflict, persecution and the redrawing of borders created waves of refugees and displaced populations on a scale the world had never seen. Migration in this era was often involuntary, driven by fear and survival, yet it also gave rise to new communities, international responses and the beginnings of a global humanitarian system.

World War I: The First Global Refugee Crisis

The First World War (1914–1918) unleashed unprecedented displacement. Entire villages were destroyed along the Western Front, forcing civilians to flee. In Eastern Europe, millions were uprooted as armies advanced and retreated. Armenians, targeted during the Ottoman Empire's genocide, were forced into death marches and exile, creating a diaspora that spread across the Middle East, Europe and the Americas.

For the first time, governments and international organisations confronted the challenge of mass refugee movements. Camps were established, aid distributed and policies debated. Migration in this era revealed the vulnerability of civilians in modern warfare.

World War II: Displacement on a Massive Scale

The Second World War (1939–1945) produced the largest refugee crisis in history. Tens of millions were displaced across Europe, Asia and Africa. Jewish communities faced the horrors of the Holocaust, with survivors scattered across the globe after liberation.

Poles, Ukrainians and other Eastern Europeans were uprooted by Nazi occupation and Soviet expansion. In Asia, millions fled Japanese invasions, while in Africa, colonial subjects were conscripted or displaced by war.

At war's end, Europe was a continent of refugees. Displaced Persons (DP) camps housed millions awaiting resettlement. Some returned home; others migrated to new lands - Australia, Canada, the United States and Israel. Migration in this era was both a tragedy and a rebirth, as survivors rebuilt lives in unfamiliar places.

Partition and Decolonisation

Beyond Europe, the mid-20th century saw migrations tied to decolonisation and the redrawing of borders. In 1947, the partition of India and Pakistan triggered one of the largest migrations in history: over 10 million people crossed borders in a matter of months, fleeing violence and seeking safety. Families carried what they could, walking along roads lined with tragedy and resilience.

Across Africa and Asia, independence movements reshaped nations. Colonial administrators departed, while new governments faced migrations of ethnic groups, workers and refugees. The end of empire was also the beginning of new diasporas, as people sought opportunity or refuge in former colonial metropoles such as London, Paris and Lisbon.

Refugees of the Cold War

The Cold War created its own migrations. Hungarians fled Soviet tanks in 1956; Czechs escaped after the Prague Spring in 1968. Vietnamese refugees, known as "boat people," fled after the fall of Saigon in 1975, risking perilous journeys across seas. Cubans crossed to Florida, East Germans tunnelled under walls and countless others sought freedom from authoritarian regimes.

These migrations highlighted the political dimension of displacement. Refugees were not only victims of war - they were symbols in ideological battles, welcomed or rejected depending on global politics.

International Responses

The scale of refugee crises in the 20th century led to new institutions. The United Nations High Commissioner for Refugees (UNHCR), founded in 1950, became a central actor in providing aid and resettlement. International conventions defined the rights of refugees and obligations of states. Migration was no longer just a national issue - it was a global responsibility.

Resettlement programs brought refugees to new homes across the world. Canada welcomed Vietnamese families; the United States admitted Eastern Europeans; Australia opened its doors to displaced persons. Migration became a story of both loss and renewal, as refugees rebuilt lives in distant lands.

The Human Dimension

Behind every statistic is a human story: a child clutching a doll while boarding a train, a family walking across a border at night, a survivor rebuilding life in a new language. War and displacement strip people of homes but migration also offers the possibility of belonging again. Refugees carry memories of loss but also dreams of future generations.

Legacy

The migrations of war and resettlement reshaped nations and identities. Diasporas grew, cultures blended and humanitarian systems evolved. Yet the challenges remain: how to protect those forced to move, how to balance compassion with politics and how to honour the resilience of those who rebuild after devastation.

Chapter 9: Modern Global Migration

The aftermath of the world wars and the dawn of the modern era ushered in a new phase of migration. Unlike the forced displacements of wartime, post-war migration was often shaped by labour demand, political agreements and the rise of nation-states with defined borders.

Millions crossed frontiers not as refugees but as workers, students and families seeking opportunity. Migration in this era became a defining feature of globalisation, reshaping societies into multicultural mosaics.

Post-War Labour Migration

In the decades after World War II, devastated economies needed rebuilding. Western Europe, in particular, faced labour shortages. Governments turned to migration to fill the gap.

> ➢ **Guest Worker Programs**: Germany recruited "Gastarbeiter" (guest workers) from Turkey, Italy and Greece. France welcomed workers from North Africa. Britain drew migrants from the Caribbean, India and Pakistan. These programs brought millions into industrial economies, transforming cities and neighbourhoods.

> ➢ **Economic Growth**: Migrants built factories, laid railroads and staffed hospitals. Their labour fuelled prosperity, while their presence reshaped cultural landscapes. Turkish kebabs, Indian curries and Caribbean music became part of European life.

Although often intended as temporary, many guest workers settled permanently, raising families and creating communities that became integral to their host nations.

Immigration Policies and Border Controls

As migration increased, governments sought to regulate it. Immigration policies became central to national debates, balancing economic needs with social concerns.

- **United States**: The Immigration and Nationality Act of 1965 abolished quotas based on nationality, opening doors to migrants from Asia, Africa and Latin America. This transformed the demographic make-up of the country, creating unprecedented diversity.

- **Europe**: Nations grappled with integration, citizenship and multiculturalism. Policies varied - some encouraged assimilation, others celebrated diversity, while still others resisted immigration altogether.

- **Global South**: Migration was not only toward the West. Countries in the Middle East, such as Saudi Arabia and the Gulf states, became magnets for labour migrants from South Asia and Africa, creating vast expatriate communities.

Borders became both gateways and barriers, shaping who could move and under what conditions. Migration was no longer just a human story - it was a political one.

The Rise of Multicultural Societies

Modern migration created societies where cultures coexisted, blended and sometimes clashed. Cities such as London, New York, Toronto and

Sydney became global hubs, where dozens of languages were spoken and traditions mingled.

> ➢ **Cultural Exchange**: Migrants brought food, music, art and religion, enriching host societies. Festivals celebrated diversity, while schools and workplaces became microcosms of global culture.
>
> ➢ **Challenges**: Integration was not always smooth. Racism, xenophobia and cultural tensions tested societies. Yet migration also sparked movements for civil rights, equality and recognition, reshaping national identities.
>
> ➢ **Diasporas**: Migrant communities maintained ties to homelands through remittances, media and travel. Diasporas became bridges between nations, linking economies and cultures across continents.

Human Stories of Modern Migration

Behind the policies and statistics are countless human journeys. A nurse from the Philippines working in London, a Moroccan family settling in Paris, a Mexican labourer crossing into California, a Somali refugee rebuilding life in Minnesota. Each story reflects resilience, adaptation and the pursuit of belonging.

Migration in the modern era is about identity as well as movement. Migrants carry traditions into new worlds, while host societies are reshaped by their presence. The result is a dynamic, ever-changing tapestry of human culture.

Globalisation and Mobility

Modern migration is inseparable from globalisation. Airplanes, telecommunications and digital networks make movement faster and easier. Students study abroad, professionals work across borders and families maintain ties through instant communication. Migration is no longer a one-way journey - it is often circular, with people moving back and forth between homelands and host countries.

Legacy

Modern global migration has created societies that are more interconnected than ever before. It has enriched cultures, fuelled economies and challenged nations to rethink identity and belonging. Yet it has also raised questions: How do we balance openness with security? How do we ensure fairness and compassion? How do we honour the contributions of migrants while addressing the tensions migration can bring?

Chapter 10: Climate, Technology and the Future of Migration

Migration has always been shaped by the forces of nature and the tools of human ingenuity. In the 21st century, those forces are accelerating. We hear that climate change is altering landscapes, rising seas are swallowing coastlines and droughts are reshaping agriculture.

At the same time, technology is transforming how people move, connect and imagine their futures. The migrations of tomorrow will be driven not only by survival but by innovation, choice and global interdependence.

Climate Change: The New Driver of Displacement

The environment has always influenced migration - ice ages, droughts and floods pushed ancient peoples to new lands. Today, climate change is emerging as one of the most powerful drivers of human movement.

➢ **Rising Seas**: Low-lying nations such as Bangladesh, the Maldives and Pacific island states could face existential threats if sea levels rise. Communities are already relocating inland, while governments debate the fate of entire populations.

➢ **Drought and Desertification**: In Africa's Sahel region, expanding deserts push farmers and herders into new territories, sparking competition and conflict. Similar pressures affect parts of the Middle East and South Asia.

➢ **Extreme Weather**: Hurricanes, floods and wildfires displace millions annually. These events, once rare, are becoming more frequent, forcing temporary and permanent migrations.

- ➢ **Food Security**: Shifts in rainfall and temperature can disrupt agriculture, compelling rural populations to move to cities or across borders in search of sustenance.

Climate migration is often involuntary, yet it is also a story of resilience. Communities adapt, governments plan and international organisations seek solutions. The future of migration will be inseparable from the future of the planet.

Technology: New Forms of Mobility

If climate change pushes people to move, technology pulls them into new forms of mobility. The digital age has transformed migration, making it faster, easier and more connected.

- ➢ **Transportation**: Air travel has shrunk the world, allowing migrants to cross continents in hours rather than months. High-speed trains and improved infrastructure make internal migration more accessible.

- ➢ **Communication**: Smart phones and the internet allow migrants to maintain ties with homelands, easing the emotional burden of distance. Social media networks guide migration decisions, sharing opportunities and risks in real time.

- ➢ **Digital Nomads**: A new form of migration has emerged - workers who move not for survival but for lifestyle. Remote work allows individuals to live in Bali, Lisbon or Mexico City while employed by companies thousands of miles away. Migration becomes a choice shaped by technology rather than necessity.

➢ **Smart Borders**: Technology also reshapes control. Biometric passports, surveillance systems and digital visas regulate movement, balancing openness with security.

Technology makes migration more fluid but it also raises questions of equity. Who has access to mobility? Who is excluded? The digital divide may determine who can move freely in the future.

Global Interdependence

Modern migration is increasingly global. Labour flows connect Asia to the Middle East, Africa to Europe, Latin America to North America. Students study abroad, professionals work across borders and families maintain transnational lives. Migration is no longer a one-way journey - it is often circular, with people moving back and forth, creating hybrid identities.

Climate change and technology intensify this interdependence. A flood in Bangladesh may send migrants to Europe; a new app may connect workers in Nairobi with employers in Dubai. Migration becomes a global system, where local events ripple across continents.

The Human Future

What will migration look like in the decades ahead? Some envision climate refugees numbering in the tens of millions, reshaping borders and politics. Others see technology enabling unprecedented freedom of movement, with individuals choosing where to live based on opportunity and lifestyle. Most likely, the future will be a blend of both - migration driven by necessity and choice, hardship and hope.

Behind these trends are human stories yet to be written: families relocating from sinking islands, young professionals working remotely across continents, communities rebuilding after disaster. Migration will remain a defining feature of humanity, as it has always been.

Continuity and Change

The future of migration is both new and ancient. Climate change and technology are novel forces, yet the underlying story is timeless: humans move to survive, to thrive and to imagine better lives. Migration will continue to shape identities, cultures and civilisations, reminding us that we are, at heart, a migratory species.

Conclusion: The Human Journey

From the first footsteps out of Africa to the crowded airports and digital networks of today, migration has been the constant thread running through human history. It is the story of survival and imagination, of hardship and hope, of leaving and belonging. Every chapter of our past has been shaped by movement - whether across deserts, oceans or city streets - and every chapter of our future will be, too.

Migration is not simply about geography. It is about identity. When people move, they carry languages, traditions and memories. They plant them in new soil, where they take root, adapt and grow. The foods we eat, the words we speak, the music we hear - all are echoes of journeys taken long before us. Migration is the great weaver of culture, binding together strands from every corner of the earth into the fabric of civilisation.

It is also about resilience. Forced migrations - through slavery, exile or war - test the limits of human endurance. Yet even in displacement, communities rebuild, preserve and transform. Diasporas become bridges between worlds, keeping alive the memory of home while shaping new identities abroad. Migration is a testament to humanity's ability to endure loss and create renewal.

And migration is about imagination. Pilgrims walk toward sacred places, explorers sail into unknown seas, workers cross borders for opportunity and refugees flee with dreams of safety. Each journey begins with a vision of life elsewhere, a belief that tomorrow can be different from today. Migration is the human capacity to imagine a better world - and the courage to pursue it.

As we look to the future, migration will remain central to our story. Climate change will push communities from vulnerable lands. Technology will enable new forms of mobility, from digital nomads to global professionals. Borders will continue to shape who can move and who cannot, raising questions of justice and compassion. Yet through it all, migration will continue to define us, as it always has.

To understand migration is to understand humanity itself. We are not a species rooted in one place - we are a species of movement, of journeys, of horizons. Our history is written in footprints across deserts, in ships crossing oceans, in caravans along trade routes and in planes soaring above continents. Migration is not the exception to human life - it is the essence of it.

The human journey is unfinished. Each migration today adds a new chapter to the story begun tens of thousands of years ago. And as long as there are horizons to cross, challenges to face and dreams to pursue, humanity will keep moving - restless, resilient and imaginative. Migration is not only our past. It is our future.

Also by Barry Richardson

Catholic Short Stories
Catholic Short Stories
Catholic Short Stories 2

Khoi-San Mythological Legacy
Cosmic Origins
Cosmic Origins 2
Trickster Tales of the Khoi-San
Rituals, Ancestors and Trance

Organic Gardening
Carbon Sequestration In Soil
Raised Bed Gardening

Short Stories
Ten Eternal Lives
The Relics That Spoke

Standalone

Before Eve

Non-Invasive Brainwave Therapy

A Concise History of Human Migration

www.ingramcontent.com/pod-product-compliance
Lightning Source LLC
LaVergne TN
LVHW090857100726
842905LV00054B/418
* 9 7 9 8 2 3 2 3 2 9 3 9 6 *